From My Mouth, To My Ears, and Into Your Heart

LEAH HUGGINS

MYND
MATTERS

Published by
Mynd Matters Publishing
715 Peachtree Street NE, Suites 100 & 200
Atlanta, GA 30308
www.myndmatterspublishing.com

978-1-948145-64-0 (pbk)

FIRST EDITION

Time's Up

In order to be fully used by God, we must come to the end of ourselves. "Then he said to the crowd, 'If any of you wants to be my follower, you must give up your own way, take up your cross daily, and follow me'" (Luke 9:23 NLT). All selfish motives must cease as we incline our ear to hear His voice and obey His instructions. We are His hands and feet, created to carry out His will on Earth. "For I did not speak from Myself, but the Father Himself, having sent Me, gave Me a commandment, what I should say and what I should speak" (John 12:49 Berean Literal Bible). The entire book of John confirms this. Are you up for the assignment? Remember, you were equipped when you were called, and you were called the day you were born. Have a fantastic day!

Reset

It is not often our desire to start over. It seems like hitting the reset button will put us farther behind. But, when handled properly, there is beauty in starting afresh. 2 Corinthians 5:17 (King James Version) says, "Therefore if any man be in Christ, he is a new creature: old things are passed away; behold, all things are become new." And Isaiah 43:18-19 (KJV) puts it like this: "Remember ye not the former things, neither consider the things of old. Behold I will do a new thing; now it shall spring fourth; shall ye not know it? I will even make a way in the wilderness, and rivers in the desert." Today, I encourage you to embrace your new thing. Don't be so attached to the past that it becomes impossible to step into the future. It's your opportunity to repaint the canvas using wisdom and knowledge.

You Are Part Of
The Plan

Your obedience to God is not contingent upon other people. Imagine how people looked at Noah when he began building the Ark (Genesis 6-9). Or the looks the prophet Hosea endured when he married Gomer, a prostitute (Hosea 1-3). Always remember, in all things, God has a plan. And we play an intricate role in the execution of His plan.

Have an awesome day!

In All Things, Trust God

In all things, I encourage you to trust God. When you're scared, trust God. When you're bold, trust God. When you're unsure, trust God. When you're confident, trust God. When you're worried, trust God. When you're nervous, excited, or anxious, trust God. In all things, trust God. Proverbs 3:5-6 (KJV) says, "Trust in the LORD with all thine heart; and lean not unto thine own understanding. In all thy ways acknowledge him, and he shall direct thy paths."

Sometimes, You Must Go Back

Recently, I was reminded that in order to move forward, sometimes we have to go back. When God revealed this to me, I asked for Scripture. He immediately reminded me of Moses. When Moses was in Egypt, he killed an Egyptian man and fled to Midian. Years later, God directed him to go back to Egypt—the same place he ran from. Now, he was not going back to "chill" with the people. He had a mission from God. He was God's mouthpiece to free the Israelites (read about it in Exodus 2-3). If God is calling you to go back, don't let your fear of the past stop you. Trust God's voice and His plan. Do what He's calling you to do. You're strong enough, you're focused enough, and you're enough to get it done.

Great Is Thy Faithfulness

I woke up this morning singing "Great is Thy Faithfulness." Seeking the Scripture for this song, I read Lamentations 3:22-24 (KJV), which says, "It is of the LORD'S mercies that we are not consumed, because his compassions fail not. They are new every morning: great is thy faithfulness. The Lord is my portion, saith my soul; therefore will I hope in him." I decided to read the entire chapter, and from what I read, the author was going through a rough time. However, he reminded himself that because of Jehovah's goodness, he's still here; living, breathing and has another chance at life. I encourage you with that today. Life may be difficult, filled with unpredictable days, but you are still here—which means God needs you...we need you. So, as you navigate this life, remember God's compassions fail not. Don't be discouraged by what happened or didn't happen yesterday. Every day is a new opportunity to get it right. He is faithful, and you're going to make it!

My Prayer for You

1 Peter 5:8 (KJV) says, "Be sober, be vigilant; because your adversary the devil, as a roaring lion, walketh about, seeking whom he may devour[.]" In this season, I pray your discernment be heightened. I pray you recognize the schemes of the enemy. I pray you do not let his tricks distract you. This is my prayer.

God = Faithful

Today I want to encourage you and remind you that our God is faithful. What He says will come to pass. And I've found that most times, things do not happen as I expected, but they happen greater than I imagined in the most unexpected way! I love how the Amplified Bible translation of Hebrews 10:23 says, "Let us seize *and* hold tightly the confession of our hope without wavering, for He who promised is reliable *and* trustworthy *and* faithful [to His word]." I challenge you to trust God to be God. He does not need a co-author. He just needs a willing vessel that will trust Him wholeheartedly. Have an awesome, trust-filled day.

Ugh! Distractions

Truth moment. Anxiety about the unknown sometimes overwhelms me. When it happens, I really want to cry. At those moments, I remember Philippians 4:6-7 (NKJV): "Be anxious for nothing, but in everything by prayer and supplication, with thanksgiving, let your requests be made known to God; and the peace of God, which surpasses all understanding, will guard your hearts and minds through Christ Jesus." But then I ask, what requests do I make known and more importantly, how did I get here? Then I realized it was a distraction, used to send me into an emotional tailspin. I shared this so you can understand how swift and subtle the enemy is. This is why it's so important to have the word of God in your heart—so you are always equipped for battle. I know God's truth concerning me, and those emotions and thoughts were not His truth. Please familiarize yourself with Scripture, and hit the enemy with the word when he attempts to rise against you. And remember you are *victorious!*

Victory or Defeat

Today, in this moment, what place are you operating from? Is it a place of victory or defeat? Romans 8:37 (KJV) says, "Nay, in all these things we are more than conquerors through him that loved us." Through Jesus, we are more than conquerors, and it's time we start acting like it. Stop believing the lies of the enemy, and rise up in the power, authority, and victory that God placed within you. It's time!

Let it Go

2 Corinthians 5:17 (KJV) says, "Therefore if any man be in Christ, he is a new creature: old things are passed away; behold, all things are become new." It's time to take off the clothes of the past that attempt to hold us back. The memories that bind us to past hurts, frustrations, and tears. It's time to free our mind and heart of those things, because they are holding us hostage and keeping us from the new thing God has ordained.

Let's let it go, sis/bruh. We've been stagnant for too long. It's time to move forward.

He is Good

Psalms 118:1 (KJV) says, "O give thanks unto the Lord; for he is good: because his mercy endureth forever." Farther down, verse 24 says, "This is the day which the Lord hath made; we will rejoice and be glad in it." Today I encourage you to remember God's goodness toward you. Even when things seem tough, God is still good. I may not be experiencing what you are, but rest assured I have my own challenges—and I continually remind myself of God's unmerited favor toward me. Remain encouraged. And know I'm praying for you. Make today a great day.

Everything God Made is Good

Genesis 1:31 (KJV) says, "And God saw everything that he had made, and, behold, it was very good. And the evening and the morning were the sixth day." Psalms 139:14 (KJV) says, "I will praise thee; for I am fearfully and wonderfully made: marvellous are thy works; and that my soul knoweth right well." God labeled us as "very good" from the beginning, and David reminds us that we are fearfully and wonderfully made. And those are just two of the many Scriptures confirming how we are viewed by Abba. So, the next time you have doubts, remember that *everything* God made is good, including you!

Shine Bright

Matthew 5:14-16 (KJV) says, "Ye are the light of the world. A city that is set on an hill cannot be hid. Neither do men light a candle, and put it under a bushel, but on a candlestick; and it giveth light unto all that are in the house. Let your light so shine before men, that they may see your good works, and glorify your Father which is in heaven." Don't try to hide or dim your light.

Shine bright!

Make Your Request Known

Philippians 4:6-7 (NKJV) says, "Be anxious for nothing, but in everything by prayer and supplication, with thanksgiving, let your requests be made known to God; and the peace of God, which surpasses all understanding, will guard your hearts and minds through Christ Jesus." It is easy to become anxious, but that anxiousness robs you of your peace. I encourage you to take a deep breath, make your request known to God, and rest as He works it out. And remember no prayer made unto God is too large, too small, or too insignificant. We are His children, and whatever concerns us concerns Him.

Run Your Race

Hebrews 12:1-2 (AMP) reads, "Therefore, since we are surrounded by so great a cloud of witnesses [who by faith have testified to the truth of God's absolute faithfulness], stripping off every unnecessary weight and the sin which so easily and cleverly entangles us, let us run with endurance and active persistence the race that is set before us, [looking away from all that will distract us and] focusing our eyes on Jesus, who is the Author and Perfecter of faith [the first incentive for our belief and the One who brings our faith to maturity], who for the joy [of accomplishing the goal] set before Him endured the cross, disregarding the shame, and sat down at the right hand of the throne of God [revealing His deity, His authority, and the completion of His work]." Don't give up. Run your race with diligence. And remember in all things you are a champion.

Silence is Not an Option

One way the enemy defeats us is by silencing us. We hear the words God has asked us to release, but due to fear we remain silent. Jeremiah 1: 4-9 (KJV) says, "Then the word of the Lord came unto me, saying, Before I formed thee in the belly I knew thee; and before thou camest forth out of the womb I sanctified thee, and I ordained thee a prophet unto the nations. Then said I, Ah, Lord God! behold, I cannot speak: for I am a child. But the Lord said unto me, Say not, I am a child: for thou shalt go to all that I shall send thee, and whatsoever I command thee thou shalt speak. Be not afraid of their faces: for I am with thee to deliver thee, saith the Lord. Then the Lord put forth his hand, and touched my mouth. And the Lord said unto me, Behold, I have put my words in thy mouth." Always remember that you are equipped. Do not allow fear to silence you. Be obedient and release the words God placed in your belly, as they have the power to deliver.

It Always Works

What do you do when life takes a totally different trajectory than you expected? We often say that we'll trust God no matter what, but sometimes, it's scary. I've been in that place several times before. Luke 22:42 (KJV) reads, "Saying, Father, if thou be willing, remove this cup from me: nevertheless, not my will, but thine, be done." God has a purpose and a plan, no matter what it looks like to us. I pray that we align with His plan. Trust His plan, no matter what it looks or feels like. In the moment, it may not make sense, but when we operate according to His plan it always works in our favor. Remain encouraged.

Have an awesome day!

One Job...Be Obedient

Through my experience, I've realized the reason I sometimes fear being obedient is my fear of the outcome. What God requests seems so significant. Why would he choose me? What if I heard him wrong? What if it doesn't work right? I'm sure Esther felt the same way when she was given the command to stand up for her people. In Esther 4:14 (KJV), Mordechai reminded her, "For if thou altogether holdest thy peace at this time, then shall there enlargement and deliverance arise to the Jews from another place; but thou and thy father's house shall be destroyed: and who knoweth whether thou art come to the kingdom for such a time as this?" The reality is God has a plan, and it is perfect. Our responsibility is to operate in obedience. We are God's vessels here on earth, and our purpose is to carry out His will. I encourage you (and myself) not to let our finite wisdom stop us from being obedient. Purpose is calling, and it's time we answer.

Worth the Wait

Today, I remind you that God's timing is perfect. Proverbs 16:9 (New International Version) says, "In their hearts humans plan their course, but the Lord establishes their steps." I often get frustrated when His promises don't happen on my timetable, but God knows exactly what we need. He will not give it to us a moment too soon. During the waiting season, I encourage you not to become anxious and truly rely on God—knowing, trusting, and believing he will do exactly what He promised. Today, I pray your patience in our Father and reliance on our Father will increase.

Take Action

Knowing what to do but not acting is destructive. James 4:17 (KJV) says, "Therefore to him that knoweth to do good, and doeth it not, to him it is sin." Remember, partial obedience is full disobedience. I encourage you not to let fear or anything else hold you captive. You are equipped. Walk in obedience. Be empowered to move forward and act today.

Living Water

John 4:7-10 (NIV) reads, "When a Samaritan woman came to draw water, Jesus said to her, 'Will you give me a drink?' (His disciples had gone into the town to buy food.) The Samaritan woman said to him, 'You are a Jew and I am a Samaritan woman. How can you ask me for a drink?' (For Jews do not associate with Samaritans.) Jesus answered her, 'If you knew the gift of God and who it is that asks you for a drink, you would have asked him and he would have given you living water.'" As you work today closing business deals, discussing corporate strategies, contemplating taking a leap of faith, or anything in this manner, I pray you allow the living water to saturate your Spirit and bring peace and restoration like never before. Have an awesome day.

Only Believe

Do you truly believe the great things God has in store for you? I mean seriously, without a shadow of a doubt, believe? If you answered honestly and sometimes struggle with this belief, it's okay. I've been there. But be careful not to dwell there. I encourage you to meditate on Jeremiah 29:11, Psalms 103, Matthew 7:7-11, and 2 Corinthians 9:8 (just to name a few). God promised an abundant life, but many times we live below this abundance because we do not truly believe it's available for us. God gives great gifts, and it's not His desire that we live anything less than abundantly. I pray you grasp the promise of His abundance and begin operating from that place and space.

It Won't Work

Attempting to fit a square peg in a round opening is comparable to being in a place where you're not assigned. No matter how desperately you try to make it work, it won't. It is not God's purpose for you to dwell in a place you were not created for. Proverbs 19:21 (NIV) says it like this: "Many are the plans in a person's heart, but it is the LORD's purpose that prevails." I encourage you not to get frustrated, but align with God's plan. Know your purpose. Surrender to it and move forward. There is so much peace and freedom there.

What are You Thinking?

What you feed your mind is what you will eventually become. If you say you are not capable, chances are, you'll never complete the task. If you say you're not worthy, you will not show up as the king/queen God designed you to be. Seriously, what are you thinking? If your thoughts do not align with Philippians 4:8, it's time for a mental reset. Let today be the genesis of a Christ-aligned mind. It's time to break the mental barriers. Let's go!

These Things

When you have time, read Romans 8. It is a powerful passage of Scripture. Romans 8:31 (KJV) asks, "What shall we then say to these things? If God be for us, who can be against us?" Have you really pondered that question? Do you speak God's word to "these things," or do you shrink back in frustration and fear? Your response to "these things" is in the same Scripture. If God be for us, who can be against us? Speak the word, stand on the word, declare the word, and watch "these things" come into alignment with the word. I encourage you to start speaking.

His Promise

Today, I encourage you not to forget God's promises toward you. Isaiah 55:11 (KJV) says, "So shall my word be that goeth forth out of my mouth: it shall not return unto me void, but it shall accomplish that which I please, and it shall prosper in the thing whereto I sent it." Even though it seems like you've been waiting for a long time, Habakkuk 2:3 (KJV) says, "For the vision is yet for an appointed time, but at the end it shall speak, and not lie: though it tarry, wait for it; because it will surely come, it will not tarry." When we feel like giving up, James 1:2-3 (AMP) encourages us with this: "Consider it nothing but joy, my brothers and sisters, whenever you fall into various trials. Be assured that the testing of your faith [through experience] produces endurance [leading to spiritual maturity, and inner peace]." Don't give up. Keep fighting. God's promises concerning you *will* come to pass.

Selah!

His Mind Didn't Change

Just because you're going through a difficult time right now, God has not changed His mind about who He created you to be. Jeremiah 1:5 (KJV) promises, "Before I formed thee in the belly I knew thee; and before thou camest forth out of the womb I sanctified thee, and I ordained thee a prophet unto the nations." Just because it seems like your life doesn't make sense doesn't negate the fact that every experience fits perfectly into your life's puzzle. Romans 8:28 (KJV) confirms, "And we know that all things work together for good to them that love God, to them who are the called according to his purpose." And just because you feel alone doesn't mean God isn't right there with you. Joshua 1:9 (English Standard Version) reminds us, "Have I not commanded you? Be strong and courageous. Do not be frightened, and do not be dismayed, for the Lord your God is with you wherever you go." Familiarize yourself with God's promises concerning your existence, and never forget that he is faithful.

Your Foundation

What foundation are you standing on? What foundation are you building your truth on? Does your truth line up with God's promise concerning you, or are you attempting to build on some randomness? Matthew 7: 24-27 (NIV) says, "Therefore everyone who hears these words of mine and puts them into practice is like a wise man who built his house on the rock. The rain came down, the streams rose, and the winds blew and beat against that house; yet it did not fall, because it had its foundation on the rock. But everyone who hears these words of mine and does not put them into practice is like a foolish man who built his house on sand. The rain came down, the streams rose, and the winds blew and beat against that house, and it fell with a great crash." Is your foundation solid? If not, it's okay. Today is a new day—the perfect day to start rebuilding according to God's solid truth.

Still Places Are Still Good

From my experience, the still places have been frustrating places. The places I've cried a lot. The places I've asked so many questions and never seemed to get answers. But today, as I sought the Lord, He took me back to Psalms 23:2-3 (NIV), which says, "He makes me lie down in green pastures, he leads me beside quiet waters, he refreshes my soul. He guides me along the right paths for his name's sake." When I surrender, it's in the still places I find rest. The tears allow me to empty myself so God can refresh my soul. Today, I encourage you to rest beside the quiet waters. Exhale frustration and inhale God's peace. Rest as He prepares you for the ministry work you're called to do. Selah.

Ripe Fruit is Better

Recently, I was in prayer concerning a situation. While everyone was voicing their opinions, I sat silently. I wanted to say something, but I wanted to provide educated commentary—an opinion that made a difference. As I prayed about it, God gently led me to Matthew 7:15-20 (NIV), which reads, "Watch out for false prophets. They come to you in sheep's clothing, but inwardly they are ferocious wolves. By their fruit you will recognize them. Do people pick grapes from thorn bushes, or figs from thistles? Likewise, every good tree bears good fruit, but a bad tree bears bad fruit. A good tree cannot bear bad fruit, and a bad tree cannot bear good fruit. Every tree that does not bear good fruit is cut down and thrown into the fire. Thus, by their fruit you will recognize them." We are so quick to act or believe, but we don't allow people's fruit to materialize. In this insta-ready time, we miss the maturation process, which is key. Today, I encourage us to slow down, sincerely seek God with our whole heart, and allow the fruit to ripen.

All Three at Once

In order for flowers to grow, there must be rain. Think about what the sky looks like when the worst storm comes through. It gets really dark. Some storms last longer than others, but the end result is the same: pretty sunshine, warm weather, or a beautiful rainbow. Maybe we experience all three at once.

Compare that to your situation. You are the flower. You don't know how long this storm will last; it may be longer, shorter, more intense, or less frustrating than the last one. Romans 8:18 (KJV) says it like this: "For I reckon that the sufferings of this present time are not worthy to be compared with the glory which shall be revealed in us." Take comfort in knowing there will be a beautiful flower who can endure the storm, enjoy the pretty sunshine, the warm weather, and the beautiful rainbow. Make it a great day.

Guard Your Thoughts

I'm sure we've all heard, "Death and life are in the power of the tongue: and they that love it shall eat the fruit thereof" (Proverbs 18:21, KJV). But did you know we start building or tearing things down with our thoughts? Whatever we think is what we start believing. This is why Paul urges us in Romans 12:2 (NIV), "Do not conform to the pattern of this world, but be transformed by the renewing of your mind. Then you will be able to test and approve what God's will is—his good, pleasing and perfect will." We must guard our thoughts, as they truly do become our actions. Have an awesome day.

You Win!

Today, I remind you that after it's all said and done, after the smoke clears, once the curtain has been drawn…you win! Although it may be tough right now, you win. Although the circumstances are not ideal, you win. Deuteronomy 20:4 (NIV) reads, "For the LORD your God is the one who goes with you to fight for you against your enemies to give you victory." Your victory is guaranteed. Always remember that. Make the remainder of this day great.

Truly, Perfectly, Authentically You

Today, I encourage you to stick to your purpose. Matthew 5:13 (The Message) reads, "Let me tell you why you are here. You're here to be salt-seasoning that brings out the God-flavors of this earth. If you lose your saltiness, how will people taste godliness? You've lost your usefulness and will end up in the garbage." You were created for a specific reason, and no one can do that like you. Do not conform to what others say you should or should not do. Be truly, perfectly, and authentically who God created you to be.

Refining Gold

Today I want to remind you that God has a perfect plan for your life. Jeremiah 29:11 (NIV) says, "'For I know the plans I have for you,' declares the LORD, 'plans to prosper you and not to harm you, plans to give you hope and a future.'" Gold smelting is the process of refining gold to remove impurities. Extreme heat and pressure are important to this process. The end result is pure gold. Now, imagine yourself as the gold and God as the gold miner. God is going to do whatever it takes to make sure you are pure, whole, and complete. Sometimes this requires fire, but the end result is worth it. Remain encouraged.

The Butterfly

Romans 8:28 (KJV) says, "And we know that all things work together for good to them that love God, to them who are the called according to his purpose." All things include the frustrating season you're currently in. When things are tough for me, I meditate on this scripture and think of the metamorphosis of a caterpillar. It begins as a fuzzy worm, but later, a beautiful butterfly emerges. We would never see the butterfly if the caterpillar abandoned the process. Be the butterfly. Have an awesome day!

Whole and Complete, Lacking Nothing

I encourage you to meditate on this Scripture as you encounter difficult situations in life: "Consider it pure joy, my brothers and sisters, whenever you face trials of many kinds, because you know that the testing of your faith produces perseverance. Let perseverance finish its work so that you may be mature and complete, not lacking anything" (James 1:2-4, NIV). Although the trials we face are a nuisance, they are important to our purpose. Know and trust that in the end, you will be whole and complete, lacking nothing.

Lean Not To Your Own Understanding

Proverbs 3:5-6 (KJV) says, "Trust in the Lord with all thine heart; and lean not unto thine own understanding. In all thy ways acknowledge him, and he shall direct thy paths." *Lean not unto thine own understanding.* I know it can get tough at times, but do not lean on your own understanding. I know the situation may even be frustrating, but do not lean on your own understanding. Lean into God and He will help you understand.

What's in Your Heart?

Psalms 119:11 (KJV) says, "Thy word have I hid in mine heart, that I might not sin against thee." What word is in your heart? Are they words of condemnation and angst, or words of praise and petition? Proverbs 4:23 (KJV) reads, "Keep thy heart with all diligence; for out of it are the issues of life." I challenge you to fill your heart with kind and uplifting words. Then, watch your actions mimic these things.

Cast Your Cares

One of the many awesome characteristics of God is His desire to handle the burdens that attempt to weigh us down. 1 Peter 5:7 (NIV) says, "Cast all your anxiety on him because he cares for you." Anxieties include fear, worries, burdens, and anything that steals your peace. Psalms 55:22 (English Standard Version) says, "Cast your burden on the LORD, and he will sustain you; he will never permit the righteous to be moved." God is imploring you to toss whatever is weighing you down to Him. Anything that takes up more space in your thoughts than God's goodness and grace should be thrown His way. He'll gladly catch it and handle it accordingly. Truthfully, you were never equipped to carry it anyway. Make this day a terrific one.

Beware of the Distraction

Today I was talking about something very dear to my heart. As I spoke, God's gentle voice reminded me not to get distracted. Then I thought about Peter walking on the water. Matthew 14:28-31 (International Standard Version) reads, "Peter answered him, 'Lord, if it's you, order me to come to you on the water.' Jesus said, 'Come on!' So, Peter got down out of the boat, started walking on the water, and came to Jesus. But when he noticed the strong wind, he was frightened. As he began to sink, he shouted, 'Lord, save me!' At once Jesus reached out his hand, caught him, and asked him, 'You who have so little faith, why did you doubt?'" Peter began to sink when he got distracted and took his eyes off Jesus. I encourage you not to lose your focus or become distracted.

You're Right, You Can't Do It

While facing a difficult situation, I said, "God I can't do this." God answered, "You're right. But I can teach you." There are many Scriptures about God teaching us, but Psalms 25:4-5 (KJV) stands out. It reads, "Shew me thy ways, O Lord; teach me thy paths. Lead me in thy truth, and teach me: for thou art the God of my salvation; on thee do I wait all the day." Today, I encourage you not to back down, but to open your heart and mind so God can teach you.

Yet Faithful

I want to remind you that God is faithful. In Numbers 23:19-20 (KJV), Balaam said, "God is not a man, that he should lie; neither the son of man, that he should repent: hath he said, and shall he not do it? or hath he spoken, and shall he not make it good? Behold, I have received commandment to bless: and he hath blessed; and I cannot reverse it." This promise still holds true today. Keep seeking, trusting, and believing what He promised. It will happen!

Be Careful with Comfort

A few years ago, out of frustration, I prayed and asked God why I can't ever get comfortable. He gently answered, "You're not supposed to get comfortable." Bewildered, I asked why, but never got a response. Years later, I said something that sparked this question again. It was then God said, "You can't get comfortable because the enemy is and will always be on attack." 1 Peter 5:8 (KJV) states, "Be sober, be vigilant; because your adversary the devil, as a roaring lion, walketh about, seeking whom he may devour:" All these years later, I finally understand why comfort is dangerous. That moment of comfort gives the enemy just enough time to attack. Stand guard and be ready always. Have a great day!

Count Up the Cost

Luke 14:28-33 (NIV) reads, "Suppose one of you wants to build a tower. Won't you first sit down and estimate the cost to see if you have enough money to complete it? For if you lay the foundation and are not able to finish it, everyone who sees it will ridicule you, saying, 'This person began to build and wasn't able to finish.' Or suppose a king is about to go to war against another king. Won't he first sit down and consider whether he is able with ten thousand men to oppose the one coming against him with twenty thousand? If he is not able, he will send a delegation while the other is still a long way off and will ask for terms of peace. In the same way, those of you who do not give up everything you have cannot be my disciples."

What is your disobedience costing you? Your joy, peace, hope, or even your health? What is it truly costing you? Is it worth it? Hebrews

3:7-11 (NLT) says, "That is why the Holy Spirit says, 'Today when you hear his voice, don't harden your hearts as Israel did when they rebelled, when they tested me in the wilderness. There your ancestors tested and tried my patience, even though they saw my miracles for forty years. So I was angry with them, and I said, 'Their hearts always turn away from me. They refuse to do what I tell them.' So in my anger I took an oath: 'They will never enter my place of rest.'" I urge you not to harden your heart toward God's instructions. It's not worth forsaking your rest, your peace, or your joy. Be obedient and carry out God's instructions. If you did harden your heart toward God's instructions, it's okay. Repent and get back in the game (I've had to do this more times than I care to admit). Have an awesome day!

His Power, Not Yours

Have you ever wondered why you're having trouble being delivered from something? No matter how hard you try, you can't stop. Or if you do stop, it's only temporary, and before you realize, you're doing it all over again? I mean, you desperately want to quit, and you're really, *really* trying, but it's not working. Could it be you're having trouble because you're attempting to do it through your own strength, your own power, your own might? 2 Corinthians 12:9 (NIV) says, "But he said to me, 'My grace is sufficient for you, for my power is made perfect in weakness.' Therefore I will boast all the more gladly about my weaknesses, so that Christ's power may rest on me." And Ephesians 3:20 (KJV) reads, "Now unto him that is able to do exceeding abundantly above all that we ask or think, according to the power that worketh in us." The real question is, what power is at work in you? Is it your power, or power from the Most High Elohim? Relinquish your power to Him and watch how things change.

Busyness of Life

Don't become so busy with life and routines that you neglect spending time with the Father. Luke 10:38-42 (NLT) reads, "As Jesus and the disciples continued on their way to Jerusalem, they came to a certain village where a woman named Martha welcomed him into her home. Her sister, Mary, sat at the Lord's feet, listening to what he taught. But Martha was distracted by the big dinner she was preparing. She came to Jesus and said, 'Lord, doesn't it seem unfair to you that my sister just sits here while I do all the work? Tell her to come and help me.' But the Lord said to her, 'My dear Martha, you are worried and upset over all these details! There is only one thing worth being concerned about. Mary has discovered it, and it will not be taken away from her.'" In this place, you'll receive guidance and direction, peace in turmoil, and rest for your soul. What you receive in this place can't be taken from you.

Trust God in All Things

Has God ever told you to pray for something, and you really wanted to, but you were afraid? After all, that same thing He placed on your heart is the same thing that hurt you. Yes, you get being obedient, and you know God has not given the spirit of fear, but you don't want to hurt anymore. You just want to forgive, heal, and move on. I am familiar with that place. But Jeremiah 29:11 (KJV) reads, "For I know the thoughts that I think toward you, saith the Lord, thoughts of peace, and not of evil, to give you an expected end." Why are you afraid to trust God? If He's telling you to do it, he has a bigger purpose. Push your fears aside and do what He's asked. You never know why God has asked you to do something; but, he did so do it. Have a great day.

Passion and Power

What place are you praying from? Is it a place of timidity or a place of power? A place of triumph or a place of loss? Hebrews 4:16 (KJV) reads, "Let us therefore come boldly unto the throne of grace, that we may obtain mercy, and find grace to help in time of need." *Come boldly.* Move with authority. Listen, the enemy is on his job—making us anxious, stealing our peace, taking our joy. Or have we given it to him because we are not on *our* job? Truth moment, Satan is real and he's on the move. We have the most effective weapon in our arsenal—prayer—but we must use it. Luke 10:19 (KJV) reads, "Behold, I give unto you power to tread on serpents and scorpions, and over all the power of the enemy: and nothing shall by any means hurt you." That's the promise. We have power to win, but we must do the work. I encourage you to begin praying with the power and passion that's inside of you. It has been dormant for too long.

Built for the Journey

Today I encourage you to trust God's plan. Trust His timeline. The wait may seem long, but it's necessary. We usually quote Jeremiah 29:11, but do we sincerely believe this passage? We don't take a cake out of the oven prematurely, or deliver a baby prior to their expected time, so why would God do anything differently with our lives? Great masterpieces take time. Maturation takes time. Remember, it's not punishment. It's protection. It's a process. Cheers to God's sovereignty and remember, you're built for this journey—your journey.

No-Thing

Not long ago I completed one of those Facebook tests. Sometimes the results are simply hilarious, but they are often accurate. This particular test revealed what I was afraid of. The result had truth to it, but it is also something I am working to overcome. As I pondered the result, Psalms 27 came to mind. Please read the entire chapter, but here's a snippet: "The Lord is my light and my salvation; whom shall I fear? the Lord is the strength of my life; of whom shall I be afraid? When the wicked, even mine enemies and my foes, came upon me to eat up my flesh, they stumbled and fell. Though an host should encamp against me, my heart shall not fear: though war should rise against me, in this will I be confident...For in the time of trouble he shall hide me in his pavilion: in the secret of his tabernacle shall he hide me; he shall set me up upon a rock" (27:1-3, 27:5 KJV). The reality is we have nothing to be afraid of. No person, situation, or circumstance. *Nothing.* God sent Jesus, and He defeated anything, everything, and all things that may rise up against us. So, yes— the Facebook test was fun, but the revelation is we truly have *nothing to fear!*

Omnipresent

The beauty of whatever difficult time you're facing is God is there with you. Many times throughout Scripture, He states He will always be wherever we are. He is omnipresent. One of my favorites is Psalms 139:7-10 (KJV), where David breaks it down. It reads, "Whither shall I go from thy spirit? or whither shall I flee from thy presence? If I ascend up into heaven, thou art there: if I make my bed in hell, behold, thou art there. If I take the wings of the morning, and dwell in the uttermost parts of the sea; Even there shall thy hand lead me, and thy right hand shall hold me." As you fight through whatever tough time you're facing, put a smile on your face knowing the Almighty is there, ushering you as you walk, protecting you as you fight, and bottling up your tears as you weep.

You're Not Forgotten

Today I remind you that God has not forgotten you. He hasn't forgotten His promise toward you. He hasn't tuned out your prayers. Isaiah 40:28-31 (NIV) reads, "Do you not know? Have you not heard? The LORD is the everlasting God, the Creator of the ends of the earth. He will not grow tired or weary, and his understanding no one can fathom. He gives strength to the weary and increases the power of the weak. Even youths grow tired and weary, and young men stumble and fall; but those who hope in the LORD will renew their strength. They will soar on wings like eagles; they will run and not grow weary, they will walk and not be faint." In this season, I pray for your strength. Strength to overcome, strength to persevere, and strength to believe. I pray for continued strength toward you and encourage you to turn your tears of anguish into tears of joy, knowing God will fulfill His promise toward you.

Turn on the light

Darkness and light; doubt and belief; fear and bravery—they cannot dwell in the same place. Matthew 6:24 (NIV) reads, "No one can serve two masters. Either you will hate the one and love the other, or you will be devoted to the one and despise the other. You cannot serve both God and money." Today, I encourage you to make a conscious decision. Your vision and dreams cannot grow in darkness, fear, or doubt. Turn on the light. Trust yourself and the vision God placed in your heart. It's time to move forward. No more stagnation. Have an awesome day!

Your Place of Love

I have a heart question for you. From what place do you love? Do you love unconditionally, or do you only love based on what you receive? If your honest answer is the latter, it's not love. John 3:16 (NIV) reads, "For God so loved the world that he gave his one and only Son, that whoever believes in him shall not perish but have eternal life." God knew we would be disobedient at times, but He made a choice to show His love, agape love, no matter how we act. I continually ask God for His guidance so I can know, embrace, understand, and navigate this part of life. I encourage you to do the same.

Why Doubt?

What if God is ready to release your desire, but you don't fully believe? You look at the outward appearance. You listen to others' opinions. You second-guess what God continually confirms. Read Matthew 14:22-34 for your answer. Doubt crept in as the disciples crossed the lake and as Peter walked on the water. Jesus soothed their fears, but He asked why they doubted. That's my question for you and for myself. Why do we doubt? Today, I encourage you to focus on the finished work—not the hiccups, detours, frustrations, and naysayers along the way. Everything God promised will come to pass, but you must believe.

Steal, Kill, Destroy

John 10:10 (NLT) states, "The thief's purpose is to steal and kill and destroy. My purpose is to give them a rich and satisfying life." Meditate on this as you go throughout your day. When things irritate you, know that's what the enemy wants—to steal your peace, your joy, your patience, and your smile. Give those nuisances to God and enjoy a peaceful, purposeful, productive day.

Peace

John 14:27 (NIV) reads, "Peace I leave with you; my peace I give you. I do not give to you as the world gives. Do not let your hearts be troubled and do not be afraid." Peace is defined as "freedom of disturbance" and it is a fruit of the Spirit. Today, I encourage you to invite peace into your heart. Speak peace to that situation. Pray peace over that person. We know "the tongue has the power of life and death, and those who love it will eat its fruit" (Proverbs 18:21, NIV). Speak peace to whatever is plaguing you and believe the situation will change. Have an awesome, peaceful day.

Celebration Time

Today, I encourage you to have a party. The purpose of this party is to celebrate your life—the good, the bad, and the ugly. We celebrate our birthdays, major accomplishments, and our loved ones celebrate our life when we transition; however, we know that every day we are alive is a blessing. Celebrate the blessing. Go to your favorite restaurant, turn on your favorite song, dance like no one's watching, or call up your laughing buddy and have a good giggle. Just do something that puts you in the mindset of celebration. Proverbs 15:15 (New American Standard Bible) reads, "All the days of the afflicted are bad, but a cheerful heart has a continual feast." And Psalms 118:24 (KJV) states, "This is the day which the LORD hath made; we will rejoice and be glad in it." So, cheers to a great celebration! You definitely deserve it.

Be Joy

Today I pray you find the strength to sift through your emotions and locate *joy.* Grasp it as if your life depends on it, because honestly, it does. Joy is a fruit of the Spirit, and we know how imperative this is to our lives. Galatians 5:22-23 (NIV) reads, "But the fruit of the Spirit is love, joy, peace, forbearance, kindness, goodness, faithfulness, gentleness and self-control. Against such things there is no law." So today, I encourage you to make a conscious decision to choose joy. *Be joyous,* and share some joy with those you come in contact with. I intentionally chose to spread joy today, and it has made a huge impact thus far.

See Past That Mountain

I want to offer a little encouragement on this beautiful day. Yes, what you're facing right now seems overwhelming and extremely difficult. But if you can see past where you are, you can see past what you see. Have the faith to dream, hope, and push forward. Mark 8:22-25 (NIV) reads, "They came to Bethsaida, and some people brought a blind man and begged Jesus to touch him. He took the blind man by the hand and led him outside the village. When he had spit on the man's eyes and put his hands on him, Jesus asked, 'Do you see anything?' He looked up and said, 'I see people; they look like trees walking around.' Once more Jesus put his hands on the man's eyes. Then his eyes were opened, his sight was restored, and he saw everything clearly." Ask Abba to restore your sight so you can see past that mountain in front of you. I pray you see clearly today.

Hidden in Plain Sight

Hebrews 13:2 (NLT) reads, "Don't forget to show hospitality to strangers, for some who have done this have entertained angels without realizing it!" In Joshua 2, God told Joshua to scout out the land, particularly around Jericho. Joshua sent spies, and word got back to the king of Jericho that spies were in Rahab's home. Rahab, a prostitute, covered for the spies and told the king they had already left the city; however, they were hidden on her roof and were able to escape. Who would have known that a prostitute, someone who was viewed as "less than," would be used to carry out God's plan? Just because a person does not look a certain way, have a particular title, or brush elbows with a certain group does not mean God has not included them to answer your prayer. Everyone has a role to play. Don't delay your freedom because it looks different than you expected. God is creative and has the solution hidden in plain sight. Trust Him and the process.

A Great Place

When it seems like life is falling apart, it's actually a sign that everything is coming together. You're in a place of complete vulnerability. In this place, God can really do what needs to be done, with no interruptions. Paul said in 2 Corinthians 12:8-10 (English Standard Version), "Three times I pleaded with the Lord about this, that it should leave me. But he said to me, 'My grace is sufficient for you, for my power is made perfect in weakness.' Therefore, I will boast all the more gladly of my weaknesses, so that the power of Christ may rest upon me. For the sake of Christ, then, I am content with weaknesses, insults, hardships, persecutions, and calamities. For when I am weak, then I am strong." So rest easy. You're in a great place. Trust the process, lay back, close your eyes, breathe, and know you're safe. I am always cheering for you.

Don't Let it Stop You

Good Friday represents the day over two thousand years ago when the same people who cried "hosanna" crucified Jesus. They did this because they did not understand Him. He was unwilling to conform, unwilling to go against His Father's instructions. Read about it in Matthew 27, Mark 15, Luke 23, or John 19. Like Jesus, people may verbally crucify you by talking down on your dreams and ambitions. Don't let that stop you. Like our elder brother Jesus, continue with the assignment God has given you. Yes, they killed Jesus, but that didn't stop him from fulfilling the task he was assigned. He's our model, so don't let naysayers and dream snatchers stop you.

Times and Seasons

Letting go and walking away from a situation is challenging, yet highly rewarding. Read Ecclesiastes 3. It speaks about the seasons in life. Sometimes we tend to hold on to situations, jobs, and relationships long after they've expired. We must make sure we keep our ears pressed to our Creator's lips so the season doesn't expire and we're caught doing an old thing in a new season. "No one sews a patch of unshrunk cloth on an old garment, for the patch will pull away from the garment, making the tear worse. Neither do people pour new wine into old wineskins. If they do, the skins will burst; the wine will run out and the wineskins will be ruined. No, they pour new wine into new wineskins, and both are preserved" (Matthew 9:16-17, NIV). Know the season, and do the work for that season.

With All Your Heart

Always remember when things hurt most, God loves us best. He holds us tighter in that situation. We have limited knowledge and may not understand why, but our all-knowing God, with his infinite power and knowledge, knows why. So today I encourage everyone to "trust in the Lord with all your heart, and do not lean on your own understanding" (Proverbs 3:5, English Standard Version). It may hurt, but trust our King to make things better. Remember the greatest lessons are learned through the toughest trials.

No Settle Zone

Scripture states, "One who is full loathes honey from the comb, but to the hungry even what is bitter tastes sweet" (Proverbs 27:7, NIV). We must make sure we remember God's promises and patiently wait for them to manifest in His time. When we rush things, often we settle—even when we know it isn't good, because we've become anxious or hungry. Let's leave the pen with the author and surrender to His timing because we know in Him we will remain full.

It's Time

"'For My thoughts are not your thoughts, nor are your ways My ways, declares the Lord. For as the heavens are higher than the earth, So, are My ways higher than your ways and My thoughts *higher* than your thoughts" (Isaiah 55:8-9, AMP). How much differently would we live our lives if we truly believed this passage? How many more faith-filled steps would we take? How would our obedience to God's instructions change? Family, it's time for us to begin living as God intended. It's time for us to move from fear to faith. It's time for us to trust God and His promises like our lives depend on it, because it does. Simply put, it's time. Have an action oriented, faith-filled day.

Don't Faint

This morning I was praying about something near and dear to my heart. As I prayed, my words quickly turned to tears. All I could say was, "God, *please* don't let me give up." Then I remembered Psalms 27:13 (King James 2000), which says, "I would have fainted, unless I had believed that I would see the goodness of the Lord in the land of the living." Although I know this is God's promise for me, I've been praying this prayer for more than ten years and it gets a bit frustrating. However, I encourage you not to faint. No matter how long you've been believing, praying, and waiting, don't faint. The next verse says, "Wait on the Lord: be of good courage, and He shall strengthen thine heart: Wait, I say, on the Lord" (Psalms 27:14, King James 2000). Be encouraged today, loved ones.

Good Promises

One day I was thinking about a particular situation. As I thought, I remembered Psalms 84:11 (KJV): "For the LORD God is a sun and shield: the LORD will give grace and glory: no good thing will he withhold from them that walk uprightly." We think we know what that "good thing" is—but when the situation does not play out as we expected, we become frustrated, sad, and depressed. God knows what His good thing is for you, and He's so gracious that He will reveal it to you if you ask and wait patiently for His response. Continue to walk upright and trust God to make good on his promises. As I always say, trust the process. I truly believe it will be worth it.

Another Chance

Today is a new day to get it right. Another chance to conquer that task, reach that goal, and pursue that dream. Another chance to try again. "I remember my affliction and my wandering, the bitterness and the gall. I well remember them, and my soul is downcast within me. Yet this I call to mind and therefore I have hope: Because of the Lord's great love we are not consumed, for his compassions never fail. They are new every morning; great is your faithfulness. I say to myself, 'The Lord is my portion; therefore, I will wait for him" (Lamentations 3: 19-24, NIV). Do not sulk in misery. The Lord afforded you another opportunity, so try, try, try again.

It's Okay

Please know it's okay to admit you are hurt, afraid, or that you don't trust the process. However, it is not okay to stay in that place. Job asked, "If I have sinned, what have I done to you, you who see everything we do? Why have you made me your target? Have I become a burden to you?" (Job 7:20, NIV). Even Jesus had questions. "And about the ninth hour Jesus cried with a loud voice, saying, Eli, Eli, lama sabachthani? that is to say, My God, my God, why hast thou forsaken me?" (Matthew 27:46, KJV). Their commonality was they took their questions to God. Job received understanding, prayed for his "friends," and came out victorious. Jesus, who knew no sin, became "that dude" who saved us all—even the ones who stoned him.

Don't act like you're not hurt, or like you have it all together when you know you're crumbling. Cry out to God. He never intended for us to handle life alone. "And the LORD, he it is that doth go before thee; he will be with thee, he will not fail thee, neither forsake thee: fear not, neither be dismayed" (Deuteronomy 31:8, KJV). And He certainly never said we would not have concerns. "I have told you these things, so that in me you may have peace. In this world you will have trouble. But take heart! I have overcome the world." (John 16:33 NIV). We must allow God to be God. It's much healthier.

Were You Created to Do That?

Recently, I purchased an item. As I was setting it up, I got frustrated because it did not perform a particular function. In that moment, God told me the item wasn't created to do that. I began to think about how often we get frustrated when we try to do things we were not created to do. Just because we're good at doing something does not necessarily mean that's what God created us to do. Knowing your purpose is imperative. "The purposes of a person's heart are deep waters, but one who has insight draws them out" (Proverbs 20:5, NIV). Ask God and He will reveal your purpose. I'm growing, but I still have a few questions concerning mine. Make today a great one.

Check Your Motives

One day I was subtly praying for something. God asked, "Why do you want that?" I answered honestly, and he replied, "No. Your motive behind that request is wrong." I laughed because He checked me quickly. "Every way of a man is right in his own eyes: but the LORD pondereth the hearts" (Proverbs 21:2, KJV). I knew I was wrong, and was still bold enough to ask because I had a point to prove. God reminded me I was in a fixed fight where I would win, but I had to get out of His way. I encourage you with that same message. You're in a fixed fight and will win; however, when you get in the way, you can really mess things up. Trust God with whatever you're battling. Wave the white flag and surrender to him. And when you pray, make sure your heart is in the right place.

The Amazing Embrace

My prayer for you today is that you feel and embrace God's unending, unfailing, *agape* love. He loves you no matter what others say or think, and that's what matters most. One night I was going through a tough time, and I prayed, "God, please hold me tonight." Honestly, it was just something I said, not really believing it would happen. But God knows what we need, and He knows our hearts' true desires. He held me that night, and the embrace I felt was amazing. Always remember, "The Lord hears his people when they call to him for help. He rescues them from all their troubles. The Lord is close to the brokenhearted; he rescues those whose spirits are crushed. The righteous person faces many troubles, but the Lord comes to the rescue each time. For the Lord protects the bones of the righteous; not one of them is broken! Calamity will surely destroy the wicked, and those who hate the righteous will be punished. But the Lord will redeem those who serve him. No one who takes refuge in him will be condemned" (Psalms 34:17-22 NLT). That's love.

Nothing Catches God Off Guard

We must always understand God has a plan. In the book of Daniel, four young men who were forcefully removed from their native Jerusalem and taken to a strange land made an everlasting impression on King Nebuchadnezzar. They completed tasks that no magician, enchanter, sorcerer, or astrologer (people in high ranking offices) could. They understood that no matter where they were or what situation they faced, God was always with them. Remain encouraged on this great day. Remember nothing catches our King off guard. He wrote the script, i.e., our life. He knew and allowed everything we've encountered, so rest easy knowing He's got you. "But don't be afraid of those who threaten you. For the time is coming when everything that is covered will be revealed, and all that is secret will be made known to all. What I tell you now in the darkness, shout abroad when daybreak comes. What I whisper in your ear, shout from the housetops for all to hear! Don't be afraid of those who want to kill your body; they cannot touch your soul. Fear only God, who can destroy both soul and body in hell. What is the price of two sparrows—one copper coin? But not a single sparrow can fall to the ground without your Father knowing it. And the very hairs on your head are all numbered. So, don't be afraid; you are more valuable to God than a whole flock of sparrows" (Matthew 10:26-31 NLT).

Partial Obedience Is Full Disobedience

Please remember partial obedience is the same as full disobedience. When God gives us a plan, we cannot pick and choose the parts we want to do and leave the other portions untouched. Proverbs, the book of wisdom, advises us to "Listen to counsel and receive instruction, That you may be wise in your latter days. There are many plans in a man's heart, Nevertheless the Lord's counsel; that will stand" (19:20-21 KNJV). We may have a plan to get things done quicker but following God's full plan—no shortcuts—is always best. Besides, there are many beautiful things and important lessons we miss by not taking God's scenic route.

By Faith

Yesterday I saw a rainbow, but it had not been raining. I thought, "That's beautiful, but strange." The prerequisite of a rainbow is rain. God reminded me that He is God, and moves as He chooses. He doesn't work according to prerequisites or man's system (I mean, He spoke *everything* into existence). If we have enough faith to believe, He can make it happen. "And by faith even Sarah, who was past childbearing age, was enabled to bear children because she considered him faithful who had made the promise" (Hebrews 11:11, NIV). I encourage you, no matter what, to not lose faith. Have a marvelous day!

The Little Red Thing

Growing up, I remember my Dad always preaching about "that little red thing in your mouth." The tongue, so small, can do the most damage. For a long time, my tongue was, and sometimes still is, my weapon—but how effective am I when I go hurt for hurt? "Likewise, the tongue is a small part of the body, but it makes great boasts. Consider what a great forest is set on fire by a small spark. The tongue also is a fire, a world of evil among the parts of the body. It corrupts the whole body, sets the whole course of one's life on fire, and is itself set on fire by hell. All kinds of animals, birds, reptiles and sea creatures are being tamed and have been tamed by mankind, but no human being can tame the tongue. It is a restless evil, full of deadly poison. With the tongue we praise our Lord and Father, and with it we curse human beings, who have been made in God's likeness. Out of the same mouth come praise and cursing. My brothers and sisters, this should not be. Can both fresh water and salt water flow from the same spring? My brothers and sisters, can a fig tree bear olives or a grapevine bear figs? Neither can a salt spring produce fresh water" (James 3:5-12, NIV). The truth is, through Christ all things are possible. Yes, even taming our tongues. Let Him be your filter, because once the words have left your mouth, you can't get them back. And sometimes, the sincerest apology is still not enough.

The To-Do List

As I was getting dressed, I thought of my to-do list. As I was going over it, God said, "That's why you get overwhelmed. Not one time did you invite me in." It's always "I have to do this or that"; never God and I. At that moment, I prayed, "God, we will tackle this project." Suddenly calm, peace, and reassurance came. "I can do all things through Christ who strengthens me" (Philippians 4:13, New King James Version). Many times, we look to friends and family for strength, but God is the one who wants to take the journey and will ensure we get to the destination. Each day I'm realizing the truth more and more—that we were created to depend and rely on Him. Let's allow Him to do His job. Grace and peace.

Gentle Reminder

Serving God is about doing things His way. I understand our way seems to be more exciting or less time-consuming, but His way is *always* the right way. "Why do you call me 'Lord, Lord,' and not do what I tell you?" (Luke 6:46, ESV). Now God, being the gentleman He is, will not force us—but it's in our best interest to be obedient. I'm not going to say it's always easy, or you won't have trials; however, His way will always work in your favor…and the benefits of doing things our King's way are amazing.

Stop Complaining

Today I was complaining and getting frustrated about a situation. As my frustration was growing, God said, "Why are you upset? I already gave you the solution. You won't move on it, so you have no right to complain." *Ouch*. How many times has God given us the answer to a situation, but for whatever reason (lack of faith, finances, time, etc.), we sit on it? "See, I have set before thee this day life and good, and death and evil; In that I command thee this day to love the Lord thy God, to walk in his ways, and to keep his commandments and his statutes and his judgments, that thou mayest live and multiply: and the Lord thy God shall bless thee in the land whither thou goest to possess it. But if thine heart turn away, so that thou wilt not hear, but shalt be drawn away, and worship other gods, and serve them; I denounce unto you this day, that ye shall surely perish, and that ye shall not prolong your days upon the land, whither thou passest over Jordan to go to possess it. I call heaven and earth to record this day against you, that I have set before you, life and death, blessing and cursing: therefore choose life, that both thou and thy seed may live: That thou mayest love the Lord thy God, and that thou mayest obey his voice, and that thou mayest cleave unto him: for he is thy life, and the length of thy days: that thou mayest dwell in the land which the Lord sware unto thy fathers, to Abraham, to Isaac, and to Jacob, to give them" (Deuteronomy 30:15-20, KJV). When we choose to obey, we are ultimately choosing life. Today I encourage you to be obedient and choose life. Have a great day!

The Small Things Count Too

I was thinking about something that I considered small, and God told me pray about it. Many times, I pray about the big stuff, but not the things I consider small. God said, "If it's on your mind and heart, it's a concern; therefore, it's important to you, and what's important to you is also important to me." Psalms 138:8 (KJV) states, "The Lord will perfect that which concerneth me: thy mercy, O Lord, endureth forever: forsake not the works of thine own hands." People always say, "don't sweat the small stuff," and they are right. Instead, add it to your prayer list.

CPSIA information can be obtained
at www.ICGtesting.com
Printed in the USA
LVHW082300050320
649180LV00019B/1092

9 781948 145763